GW01606947

Published by Geddes & Grosset Ltd,
New Lanark, Scotland.

ISBN 1 85534 160 3

Printed and bound in UK

10 9 8 7 6 5 4 3 2

Jesus Calls his Disciples

Retold by Judy Hamilton
Illustrated by Lindsay Duff

Tarantula Books

Jesus stayed with his mother Mary in Nazareth until he was thirty. But the time came when Jesus had to leave to do the work that God had sent him to earth for.

Jesus had heard of a man called John the Baptist and wished to see him. John had been preaching about God for a long time, and when he had taught people about God and they believed in him, John would baptise them in the river, giving them a sign that they had been washed free of sin. John knew that a Saviour was coming and had been telling the people to whom he preached of his coming. When Jesus came to him at last, John knew at once who he was.

"Behold, the Lamb of God!" he cried.

Jesus asked John to baptise him. God had sent him to earth as a man, and he wanted to be baptised as any other man. John, feeling too lowly for such a task, at first refused, saying to Jesus:

"I need to be baptised by you."

But finally, he realized that this was what Jesus really wanted, so he led him down to the river. And when Jesus had been baptised, a great light from Heaven shone down, and John heard God speaking:

"This is my beloved Son, in whom I am well pleased."

When Jesus had left him, John carried on with his preaching. And now he could tell people that he had seen the Saviour and had heard God speak, naming Jesus as his beloved son.

One of the people who heard John the Baptist talk about Jesus was a man called Andrew, a fisherman. Andrew had a brother called Simon who worked beside him. The brothers had two friends, also fishermen, with whom they often sailed.

One day, when Jesus had been teaching in Galilee, he came upon Simon and Andrew by the seashore. They were standing with James and John beside their boats, mending their nets. Jesus went up to them and, stepping into Simon's boat, asked them if they would take him out on the water, so that he could preach to the people who had gathered on the shore.

The men gladly agreed. They stayed close enough to the shore for Jesus to be able to talk to the people, and this he did for quite a long time.

When Jesus had finished preaching, he asked Simon to take his boat out into deeper water. Simon did this, but when Jesus asked him to lower his fishing net into the water, he was puzzled.

"Master, we have worked all night and have not caught anything. But if you wish, I will let down the net," he said.

So saying, Simon and Andrew unfolded the fishing net and let it down into the water.

The brothers were quite astounded to find that the net filled up with fish very quickly, and they had to call for James and John to come to help.

The four men hauled in so much fish that the two boats were beginning to sink. The fishermen were frightened and knelt down before Jesus.

They felt that they were not good enough to be in the company of Jesus.

Jesus spoke to the four men gently.

"Fear not," he told them. "From now on, you shall catch men."

In this way, Jesus told the four men to come with him as his disciples, calling others in the world to follow the Lord. Jesus gave Simon another name, Peter, which means 'stone'. He knew that in the years after his death, Peter would be the rock upon which Christianity was built.

Soon, Jesus called eight other men to follow him; Philip, Bartholomew, Matthew, Thomas, James, son of Alphaeus, Simon, Judas, brother of James, and Judas Iscariot. Under the guidance of Jesus, these twelve men helped Jesus with God's work for him, and were his constant companions for the rest of his life on earth. And after Jesus was crucified, it was the work of his disciples that carried the news of the Saviour round the world for all to hear.

In the years that they spent in his company, the disciples were to learn many lessons from Jesus. He taught them about the power of love, the virtue of humility, the evils of greed and envy, and many more things. And throughout their lives, the disciples worked gladly to pass these teachings on to others.

But not all of the lessons that the disciples learnt were taught to them through the words that Jesus said. Sometimes they had to be shown.

And so it happened that one evening the disciples learnt an important lesson about trust.

The twelve men had already been with their master for some time. They had seen him heal many people of their diseases and had heard him preach in many places.

On this particular day, Jesus had been teaching crowds of people and healing the sick for many hours, and as day wore on into evening, he became very tired.

He walked down to the water's edge and, stepping into a boat, he asked his disciples to take the boat out onto the water. He wanted to cross to the other side of the lake.

The disciples pushed the boat off the beach and into the water, then, stepping in beside their master, they set sail across the calm waters.

Jesus settled himself down at the back of the boat. Lulled by the gentle movements of the vessel and worn out by his labours, he soon fell asleep.

They had not gone far out into the lake when the disciples could see signs that a storm was coming. The sky darkened, and the gentle breeze began to grow stronger.

The disciples felt uneasy. They were unsure whether they should turn back or carry on and hope that they would get to the other side of the lake before the storm broke. But Jesus was sleeping, and they did not want to wake him and ask him.

They carried on sailing, watching the sky with concern as the waves began to grow bigger and the boat began to rock.

Suddenly, the weather began to get much worse. The rain came lashing down and the wind became very fierce. The waves crashed against the side of the boat with increasing strength.

Before long, they were in the grip of a full-blown storm, and the wind was tossing the little ship from side to side. The crashing waves grew higher and higher, and the disciples began to become very frightened.

Through all this, Jesus slept on.

The waves were battering the ship as though they might break it. The boat was beginning to fill up with water.

The disciples, who knew the dangers of storms at sea, began to fear for their lives.

And still Jesus continued to sleep peacefully.

Finally, the disciples became so frightened that they went to wake Jesus.

"Save us, Lord!" they begged. "We are dying!"

Jesus woke, and seeing the frightened men around him, stood up in the boat.

He held up his hand and spoke to the wind and the waves, saying:

"Peace. Be still."

At once, the wind died down and the waves stopped crashing against the boat. In no time at all, all was calm and once more the boat bobbed gently on a calm sea.

Jesus turned to his disciples. He was disappointed in them.

"Why are you so fearful?" he said to them. "How is it that you have no faith?"

The disciples should have known that while they were with Jesus, he was looking after them and no harm could come to them. They should have trusted him to keep them safe, no matter how bad things appeared to be.

The disciples were amazed by what they had seen.

"What kind of man is this, that even the wind and the sea obey him?" they asked themselves.

But they had learnt their lesson well.

Whatever happened, they should know that they could trust Jesus absolutely. If they did this, they would have nothing to fear.